All About Feelings

MY FIRST MANNERS

Written by Sarah Albee

Illustrated by Tom Brannon

Published by Phoenix International Publications, Inc.
8501 West Higgins Road, Suite 300, Chicago, Illinois 60631
Lower Ground Floor, 59 Gloucester Place, London W1U 8JJ

www.pikidsmedia.com

p i kids is a trademark of Phoenix International Publications, Inc., and is registered in the United States.

8 7 6 5 4 3 2 1

ISBN3: 978-1-4127-6782-8

phoenix international publications, inc.

Today is Big Bird's birthday!
How do you think he feels?

sleepy   mad   excited

Big Bird feels **excited**!

"Elmo, will you come over to celebrate my birthday with me?" asks Big Bird.
But Elmo says he's not feeling very well.
How do you think Big Bird feels now?

giggly   sad   afraid

Big Bird feels **sad**.

Then Big Bird sees Ernie and Bert. "Hi guys!
Do you want to play with me?"
"Sorry!" says Bert. "We're going to a party!"
How do you think Big Bird feels now?

mad   dizzy   proud

Big Bird feels **mad**!

Next, Big Bird asks his friend Zoe to come over.
But Zoe says she has a trombone lesson.
"I didn't know you played the trombone,"
says Big Bird. How do you think Big Bird feels now?

confused   giggly   silly

Big Bird feels **confused**!

"Oh, dear," Big Bird says to himself.
"What if nobody comes over for my birthday?"
How do you think Big Bird feels now?

worried   excited   sleepy

Big Bird feels **worried**.

Some little birdies are tugging on Big Bird's feathers. They want him to come around the corner. "What's going on?" wonders Big Bird. "Hey! All of my friends are here!" How do you think Big Bird feels now?

surprised   proud   dizzy

Big Bird feels **surprised**!

All of Big Bird's friends have planned
this surprise party for him!
How do you think Big Bird feels now?

sorry

happy

angry

You guessed it.
He feels **happy**!
"Happy birthday, Big Bird!"